50 Delicious Bread Dishes for Home

By: Kelly Johnson

Table of Contents

- Classic White Bread
- Whole Wheat Bread
- French Baguette
- Sourdough Bread
- Brioche
- Cinnamon Rolls
- Garlic Bread
- Focaccia
- Challah
- Banana Bread
- Zucchini Bread
- Irish Soda Bread
- Multigrain Bread
- Soft Dinner Rolls
- Pizza Dough
- Pita Bread
- Naan
- Ciabatta
- Bagels

- English Muffins
- Sweet Potato Bread
- Honey Wheat Bread
- Pumpkin Bread
- Rye Bread
- Cornbread
- Pretzels
- Flatbread
- Pumpernickel Bread
- Amish White Bread
- Artisan Bread
- Herb Bread
- Sweet Brioche Rolls
- Lemon Bread
- Cheese Bread
- Olive Bread
- Apple Cinnamon Bread
- Egg Bread
- Anadama Bread
- Bialys
- Lavash

- Empanada Dough
- Cresent Rolls
- Brioche Hamburger Buns
- Fougasse
- Rye Rolls
- Chocolate Babka
- Apple Bread
- Multigrain Rolls
- Gluten-Free Bread
- Avocado Toast Bread

Classic White Bread

Ingredients:

- 3 1/4 cups (410g) all-purpose flour
- 2 tbsp sugar
- 2 tsp salt
- 1 packet (2 1/4 tsp) active dry yeast
- 1 1/4 cups (300ml) warm water
- 2 tbsp unsalted butter, softened

Instructions:

1. In a large bowl, combine flour, sugar, salt, and yeast.
2. Add warm water and butter, then stir until the dough comes together.
3. Knead the dough on a lightly floured surface for 8-10 minutes until smooth and elastic.
4. Place the dough in a greased bowl, cover with a damp cloth, and let rise in a warm place for 1-2 hours or until doubled in size.
5. Preheat oven to 375°F (190°C). Punch down the dough, shape it into a loaf, and place it in a greased 9x5-inch loaf pan.
6. Let rise for 30-45 minutes.
7. Bake for 25-30 minutes or until golden brown. Let cool before slicing.

Whole Wheat Bread

Ingredients:

- 2 cups (250g) whole wheat flour
- 1 1/2 cups (190g) all-purpose flour
- 1 packet (2 1/4 tsp) active dry yeast
- 1 tbsp honey
- 1 tsp salt
- 1 1/4 cups (300ml) warm water
- 2 tbsp olive oil

Instructions:

1. In a bowl, combine whole wheat flour, all-purpose flour, yeast, and salt.
2. Add warm water, honey, and olive oil. Stir until the dough comes together.
3. Knead the dough for 8-10 minutes until smooth and elastic.
4. Place the dough in a greased bowl, cover, and let rise for 1-2 hours.
5. Preheat oven to 375°F (190°C). Punch down the dough and shape it into a loaf.
6. Place the dough in a greased loaf pan and let rise for 30-45 minutes.
7. Bake for 25-30 minutes or until the bread sounds hollow when tapped. Let cool before slicing.

French Baguette

Ingredients:

- 3 1/2 cups (440g) all-purpose flour
- 1 1/2 tsp salt
- 1 packet (2 1/4 tsp) active dry yeast
- 1 1/4 cups (300ml) warm water

Instructions:

1. In a large bowl, combine flour, salt, and yeast.
2. Add warm water and stir until the dough forms.
3. Knead the dough for 8-10 minutes until smooth.
4. Place the dough in a greased bowl, cover with a cloth, and let rise for 1-2 hours.
5. Preheat oven to 475°F (245°C). Punch down the dough and divide it into 2 equal portions.
6. Shape each portion into a baguette and place on a baking sheet lined with parchment paper.
7. Let rise for 30-45 minutes.
8. Use a sharp knife to make slashes on the top of each baguette.
9. Bake for 20-25 minutes until golden and crispy. Let cool before slicing.

Sourdough Bread

Ingredients:

- 3 cups (375g) all-purpose flour
- 1 cup (125g) sourdough starter
- 1 1/4 cups (300ml) warm water
- 2 tsp salt

Instructions:

1. In a large bowl, combine flour and salt.
2. Add sourdough starter and warm water, then mix until the dough comes together.
3. Knead the dough for 8-10 minutes until smooth and elastic.
4. Place the dough in a greased bowl, cover, and let rise for 4-6 hours or overnight.
5. Preheat oven to 475°F (245°C). Punch down the dough and shape it into a round loaf.
6. Place the dough onto a baking sheet lined with parchment paper and let it rise for 1 hour.
7. Bake for 30-35 minutes until the bread sounds hollow when tapped. Let cool before slicing.

Brioche

Ingredients:

- 3 1/4 cups (400g) all-purpose flour
- 1/4 cup (50g) sugar
- 1 tsp salt
- 1 packet (2 1/4 tsp) active dry yeast
- 5 large eggs
- 1 cup (230g) unsalted butter, softened
- 1/4 cup (60ml) warm milk

Instructions:

1. In a large bowl, combine flour, sugar, salt, and yeast.
2. Add eggs and warm milk, then mix until the dough comes together.
3. Knead the dough for 10-15 minutes, adding butter gradually, until smooth and elastic.
4. Place the dough in a greased bowl, cover, and let rise for 2 hours.
5. Preheat oven to 375°F (190°C). Punch down the dough and shape it into a loaf.
6. Place in a greased loaf pan and let rise for 1 hour.
7. Bake for 25-30 minutes or until golden brown. Let cool before slicing.

Cinnamon Rolls

Ingredients:

- 4 cups (500g) all-purpose flour
- 1 packet (2 1/4 tsp) active dry yeast
- 1/2 cup (100g) sugar
- 1/2 cup (120ml) milk, warmed
- 1/2 cup (115g) unsalted butter, softened
- 2 eggs
- 1/2 tsp salt

For the Filling:

- 1/2 cup (115g) unsalted butter, softened
- 1 cup (200g) brown sugar
- 2 tbsp ground cinnamon

For the Glaze:

- 1 cup (120g) powdered sugar
- 1-2 tbsp milk
- 1/2 tsp vanilla extract

Instructions:

1. In a bowl, combine flour, yeast, sugar, and salt.
2. Add warm milk, butter, and eggs, then stir until a dough forms.
3. Knead the dough for 8-10 minutes until smooth.

4. Place in a greased bowl, cover, and let rise for 1-2 hours.

5. Preheat oven to 375°F (190°C). Punch down the dough and roll it out into a rectangle.

6. Spread softened butter over the dough, then sprinkle with brown sugar and cinnamon.

7. Roll the dough into a log, cut into 12 rolls, and place them on a greased baking dish.

8. Let rise for 30-45 minutes.

9. Bake for 20-25 minutes until golden.

10. For the glaze, mix powdered sugar, milk, and vanilla extract. Drizzle over the warm rolls.

Garlic Bread

Ingredients:

- 1 loaf of French baguette or Italian bread
- 1/2 cup (115g) unsalted butter, softened
- 3-4 garlic cloves, minced
- 1 tbsp fresh parsley, chopped
- 1/2 tsp salt

Instructions:

1. Preheat oven to 375°F (190°C).
2. Slice the bread in half lengthwise.
3. In a bowl, mix butter, garlic, parsley, and salt.
4. Spread the garlic butter mixture evenly on the cut sides of the bread.
5. Place the bread on a baking sheet and bake for 10-12 minutes, or until golden.
6. Slice and serve warm.

Focaccia

Ingredients:

- 4 cups (500g) all-purpose flour
- 1 packet (2 1/4 tsp) active dry yeast
- 1 1/2 cups (360ml) warm water
- 1/4 cup (60ml) olive oil
- 1 tsp salt
- 1 tbsp fresh rosemary, chopped

Instructions:

1. In a bowl, combine flour, yeast, and salt.
2. Add warm water and olive oil, then mix until the dough comes together.
3. Knead the dough for 8-10 minutes until smooth.
4. Place the dough in a greased bowl, cover, and let rise for 1-2 hours.
5. Preheat oven to 400°F (200°C).
6. Punch down the dough, shape it into a rectangle, and place it on a greased baking sheet.
7. Press your fingers into the dough to create dimples.
8. Drizzle with olive oil and sprinkle with rosemary.
9. Bake for 20-25 minutes until golden. Let cool before slicing.

Challah

Ingredients:

- 4 cups (500g) all-purpose flour
- 1 packet (2 1/4 tsp) active dry yeast
- 1/4 cup (50g) sugar
- 1 tsp salt
- 1 cup (240ml) warm water
- 1/4 cup (60ml) vegetable oil
- 3 large eggs

Instructions:

1. In a bowl, combine flour, yeast, sugar, and salt.
2. Add warm water, oil, and eggs, then mix to form dough.
3. Knead for 8-10 minutes until smooth.
4. Place dough in a greased bowl, cover, and let rise for 1-2 hours.
5. Preheat oven to 375°F (190°C).
6. Punch down the dough and divide into 3 portions. Braid the portions together and form a loaf.
7. Place the dough on a greased baking sheet and let rise for 30-45 minutes.
8. Bake for 25-30 minutes or until golden. Let cool before slicing.

Banana Bread

Ingredients:

- 2-3 ripe bananas, mashed
- 1/3 cup (75g) melted butter
- 1 tsp baking soda
- 1/4 tsp salt
- 3/4 cup (150g) sugar
- 1 large egg, beaten
- 1 tsp vanilla extract
- 1 1/2 cups (190g) all-purpose flour

Instructions:

1. Preheat oven to 350°F (175°C). Grease a 9x5-inch loaf pan.
2. In a bowl, mix mashed bananas and melted butter.
3. Stir in baking soda, salt, sugar, egg, and vanilla.
4. Add flour and mix until just combined.
5. Pour the batter into the prepared pan.
6. Bake for 60-65 minutes, or until a toothpick comes out clean. Let cool before slicing.

Zucchini Bread

Ingredients:

- 2 cups (250g) all-purpose flour
- 1 1/2 tsp baking soda
- 1/2 tsp baking powder
- 1 tsp ground cinnamon
- 1/2 tsp salt
- 2 large eggs
- 1 cup (200g) sugar
- 1/2 cup (120ml) vegetable oil
- 1 tsp vanilla extract
- 1 1/2 cups (150g) grated zucchini
- 1/2 cup (50g) chopped walnuts or pecans (optional)

Instructions:

1. Preheat oven to 350°F (175°C) and grease a 9x5-inch loaf pan.
2. In a bowl, whisk together flour, baking soda, baking powder, cinnamon, and salt.
3. In another bowl, beat the eggs and sugar until smooth. Add oil and vanilla, mixing until combined.
4. Stir in the grated zucchini and nuts (if using).
5. Gradually fold in the dry ingredients, mixing until just combined.
6. Pour the batter into the prepared pan and bake for 55-65 minutes or until a toothpick comes out clean. Let cool before slicing.

Irish Soda Bread

Ingredients:

- 3 cups (375g) all-purpose flour
- 1 tsp baking soda
- 1 tsp salt
- 1 1/4 cups (300ml) buttermilk

Instructions:

1. Preheat oven to 425°F (220°C) and line a baking sheet with parchment paper.
2. In a large bowl, whisk together flour, baking soda, and salt.
3. Gradually pour in the buttermilk, mixing with a wooden spoon until the dough comes together.
4. Turn the dough out onto a lightly floured surface and knead gently 3-4 times.
5. Shape the dough into a round loaf and place it on the prepared baking sheet.
6. Use a sharp knife to cut a cross on top of the dough.
7. Bake for 35-45 minutes or until golden and hollow-sounding when tapped on the bottom. Let cool before slicing.

Multigrain Bread

Ingredients:

- 2 cups (250g) whole wheat flour
- 1 cup (125g) all-purpose flour
- 1/2 cup (45g) rolled oats
- 1/4 cup (30g) sunflower seeds
- 1/4 cup (30g) flax seeds
- 1 packet (2 1/4 tsp) active dry yeast
- 1 tsp salt
- 1 tbsp honey
- 1 1/4 cups (300ml) warm water

Instructions:

1. In a large bowl, combine whole wheat flour, all-purpose flour, oats, sunflower seeds, flax seeds, yeast, and salt.
2. Add honey and warm water, stirring until the dough comes together.
3. Knead the dough for 8-10 minutes until smooth and elastic.
4. Place in a greased bowl, cover, and let rise for 1-2 hours or until doubled in size.
5. Preheat oven to 375°F (190°C). Punch down the dough, shape into a loaf, and place it in a greased 9x5-inch pan.
6. Let rise for 30-45 minutes.
7. Bake for 30-35 minutes or until golden and hollow-sounding when tapped. Let cool before slicing.

Soft Dinner Rolls

Ingredients:

- 3 cups (375g) all-purpose flour
- 1 packet (2 1/4 tsp) active dry yeast
- 1/4 cup (50g) sugar
- 1/2 tsp salt
- 1/2 cup (120ml) warm milk
- 1/4 cup (60g) unsalted butter, softened
- 2 large eggs

Instructions:

1. In a bowl, combine flour, yeast, sugar, and salt.
2. Add warm milk, butter, and eggs. Stir until the dough comes together.
3. Knead the dough for 8-10 minutes until smooth and elastic.
4. Place dough in a greased bowl, cover, and let rise for 1-2 hours.
5. Preheat oven to 375°F (190°C). Punch down the dough and divide into 12 equal pieces.
6. Shape each piece into a roll and place on a greased baking sheet.
7. Let rise for 30-45 minutes.
8. Bake for 12-15 minutes or until golden brown. Let cool before serving.

Pizza Dough

Ingredients:

- 2 1/4 cups (280g) all-purpose flour
- 1 packet (2 1/4 tsp) active dry yeast
- 1 tsp sugar
- 1 tsp salt
- 3/4 cup (180ml) warm water
- 1 tbsp olive oil

Instructions:

1. In a bowl, combine flour, yeast, sugar, and salt.
2. Add warm water and olive oil, stirring until the dough comes together.
3. Knead for 8-10 minutes until smooth.
4. Place the dough in a greased bowl, cover, and let rise for 1-2 hours.
5. Preheat oven to 475°F (245°C). Punch down the dough and divide into 2 portions.
6. Roll each portion into a round pizza shape and top with your favorite toppings.
7. Bake for 10-12 minutes until the crust is golden and the cheese is bubbly.

Pita Bread

Ingredients:

- 2 1/2 cups (310g) all-purpose flour
- 1 packet (2 1/4 tsp) active dry yeast
- 1 tsp salt
- 1 tbsp olive oil
- 3/4 cup (180ml) warm water

Instructions:

1. In a bowl, combine flour, yeast, and salt.
2. Add olive oil and warm water, mixing until the dough forms.
3. Knead the dough for 8-10 minutes until smooth.
4. Place the dough in a greased bowl, cover, and let rise for 1-2 hours.
5. Preheat oven to 475°F (245°C) and place a baking sheet in the oven to heat.
6. Punch down the dough and divide into 6 equal portions. Roll each into a ball, then flatten into circles.
7. Place the dough on the preheated baking sheet and bake for 5-7 minutes, until puffy and golden.
8. Let cool before serving.

Naan

Ingredients:

- 2 cups (250g) all-purpose flour
- 1 packet (2 1/4 tsp) active dry yeast
- 1 tsp sugar
- 1 tsp salt
- 1/2 cup (120ml) warm milk
- 2 tbsp plain yogurt
- 2 tbsp olive oil

Instructions:

1. In a bowl, combine flour, yeast, sugar, and salt.
2. Add warm milk, yogurt, and olive oil, mixing until the dough comes together.
3. Knead for 8-10 minutes until smooth.
4. Place the dough in a greased bowl, cover, and let rise for 1-2 hours.
5. Preheat a skillet or griddle over medium-high heat.
6. Punch down the dough and divide into 6 equal pieces. Roll each into an oval shape.
7. Cook each piece of dough in the skillet for 2-3 minutes per side, until golden brown and puffy. Serve warm.

Ciabatta

Ingredients:

- 3 1/2 cups (440g) all-purpose flour
- 1 1/2 tsp salt
- 1 packet (2 1/4 tsp) active dry yeast
- 1 1/2 cups (360ml) warm water
- 2 tbsp olive oil

Instructions:

1. In a large bowl, combine flour, salt, and yeast.
2. Add warm water and olive oil, stirring until the dough comes together.
3. Knead the dough for 10-12 minutes until smooth.
4. Place the dough in a greased bowl, cover, and let rise for 1-2 hours.
5. Preheat oven to 475°F (245°C) and place a baking sheet in the oven.
6. Punch down the dough, shape it into an oblong loaf, and place it on a parchment-lined baking sheet.
7. Let rise for 30 minutes.
8. Bake for 20-25 minutes until golden and hollow-sounding when tapped. Let cool before slicing.

Bagels

Ingredients:

- 4 cups (500g) all-purpose flour
- 1 packet (2 1/4 tsp) active dry yeast
- 1 tbsp sugar
- 1 tsp salt
- 1 1/2 cups (360ml) warm water
- 1 tbsp olive oil
- 1 tbsp malt syrup (optional for boiling)

Instructions:

1. In a large bowl, combine flour, yeast, sugar, and salt.
2. Add warm water and olive oil, stirring until the dough comes together.
3. Knead the dough for 8-10 minutes until smooth.
4. Place the dough in a greased bowl, cover, and let rise for 1 hour.
5. Preheat oven to 425°F (220°C).
6. Punch down the dough, divide into 8 equal pieces, and roll each into a ball.
7. Use your finger to make a hole in the center of each ball, stretching it into a ring shape.
8. Bring a large pot of water to a boil and add malt syrup (if using). Boil each bagel for 1 minute per side.
9. Place the boiled bagels on a baking sheet and bake for 15-20 minutes until golden. Let cool before serving.

English Muffins

Ingredients:

- 2 1/4 cups (280g) all-purpose flour
- 1 packet (2 1/4 tsp) active dry yeast
- 1 tsp sugar
- 1/2 tsp salt
- 3/4 cup (180ml) warm milk
- 2 tbsp butter, melted
- Cornmeal for dusting

Instructions:

1. In a bowl, combine flour, yeast, sugar, and salt.
2. Add warm milk and melted butter, mixing until the dough comes together.
3. Knead the dough for 8-10 minutes until smooth.
4. Place the dough in a greased bowl, cover, and let rise for 1 hour or until doubled in size.
5. Preheat a griddle or skillet over medium heat.
6. Punch down the dough and divide it into 8 equal portions. Shape each portion into a round disc.
7. Dust a baking sheet with cornmeal and place the muffins on it. Let them rise for 30 minutes.
8. Cook each muffin on the griddle for 5-7 minutes per side, until golden brown. Let cool before serving.

Sweet Potato Bread

Ingredients:

- 1 1/2 cups (180g) all-purpose flour
- 1 tsp baking powder
- 1/2 tsp baking soda
- 1 tsp ground cinnamon
- 1/2 tsp ground nutmeg
- 1/4 tsp salt
- 1 cup (200g) mashed sweet potato
- 1/2 cup (120ml) vegetable oil
- 1/2 cup (100g) brown sugar
- 2 large eggs
- 1 tsp vanilla extract

Instructions:

1. Preheat oven to 350°F (175°C) and grease a loaf pan.
2. In a bowl, whisk together flour, baking powder, baking soda, cinnamon, nutmeg, and salt.
3. In another bowl, mix together mashed sweet potato, oil, brown sugar, eggs, and vanilla extract.
4. Gradually add the dry ingredients to the wet ingredients, stirring until combined.
5. Pour the batter into the prepared loaf pan and bake for 55-65 minutes, or until a toothpick inserted comes out clean.
6. Let cool before slicing.

Honey Wheat Bread

Ingredients:

- 2 cups (250g) whole wheat flour
- 1 1/2 cups (180g) all-purpose flour
- 1 packet (2 1/4 tsp) active dry yeast
- 1/4 cup (60ml) warm water
- 1/4 cup (60ml) honey
- 1 tsp salt
- 1/4 cup (60ml) vegetable oil
- 3/4 cup (180ml) warm milk

Instructions:

1. In a bowl, combine yeast, warm water, and honey. Let sit for 5 minutes, until foamy.
2. Add the milk, oil, salt, and flours. Stir to combine.
3. Knead the dough for 8-10 minutes until smooth and elastic.
4. Place the dough in a greased bowl, cover, and let rise for 1 hour or until doubled in size.
5. Punch down the dough and shape it into a loaf.
6. Place the dough in a greased loaf pan and let it rise for 30-45 minutes.
7. Preheat oven to 350°F (175°C) and bake for 30-35 minutes until golden brown. Let cool before slicing.

Pumpkin Bread

Ingredients:

- 2 cups (250g) all-purpose flour
- 1 tsp baking soda
- 1/2 tsp baking powder
- 1 tsp ground cinnamon
- 1/2 tsp ground nutmeg
- 1/4 tsp salt
- 1 1/2 cups (350g) pumpkin puree
- 1/2 cup (100g) sugar
- 1/2 cup (120ml) vegetable oil
- 2 large eggs
- 1 tsp vanilla extract

Instructions:

1. Preheat oven to 350°F (175°C) and grease a loaf pan.
2. In a bowl, whisk together flour, baking soda, baking powder, cinnamon, nutmeg, and salt.
3. In another bowl, combine pumpkin, sugar, oil, eggs, and vanilla.
4. Gradually add the dry ingredients to the wet ingredients, stirring until combined.
5. Pour the batter into the prepared loaf pan and bake for 60-70 minutes or until a toothpick inserted comes out clean.
6. Let cool before slicing.

Rye Bread

Ingredients:

- 2 cups (250g) rye flour
- 2 cups (250g) all-purpose flour
- 1 packet (2 1/4 tsp) active dry yeast
- 1 1/2 cups (360ml) warm water
- 1 tbsp sugar
- 1 1/2 tsp salt
- 1 tbsp vegetable oil

Instructions:

1. In a bowl, combine both types of flour, yeast, sugar, and salt.
2. Add warm water and oil, mixing until the dough comes together.
3. Knead the dough for 8-10 minutes until smooth.
4. Place the dough in a greased bowl, cover, and let rise for 1-2 hours.
5. Punch down the dough and shape it into a loaf.
6. Place it in a greased loaf pan and let rise for 30-45 minutes.
7. Preheat oven to 375°F (190°C) and bake for 30-35 minutes. Let cool before slicing.

Cornbread

Ingredients:

- 1 cup (120g) cornmeal
- 1 cup (120g) all-purpose flour
- 1/4 cup (50g) sugar
- 1 tbsp baking powder
- 1/2 tsp salt
- 1 cup (240ml) milk
- 2 large eggs
- 1/4 cup (60g) melted butter

Instructions:

1. Preheat oven to 400°F (200°C) and grease a baking dish or skillet.
2. In a bowl, combine cornmeal, flour, sugar, baking powder, and salt.
3. In another bowl, whisk together milk, eggs, and melted butter.
4. Add the wet ingredients to the dry ingredients, stirring until combined.
5. Pour the batter into the prepared pan and bake for 20-25 minutes until golden brown. Let cool before serving.

Pretzels

Ingredients:

- 2 1/2 cups (310g) all-purpose flour
- 1 packet (2 1/4 tsp) active dry yeast
- 1 tsp sugar
- 1 tsp salt
- 1 cup (240ml) warm water
- 10 cups (2.5L) water (for boiling)
- 1/4 cup (60g) baking soda

Instructions:

1. In a bowl, combine flour, yeast, sugar, and salt.
2. Add warm water and knead the dough for 8-10 minutes until smooth.
3. Place the dough in a greased bowl, cover, and let rise for 1 hour.
4. Preheat oven to 450°F (230°C) and line a baking sheet with parchment paper.
5. Punch down the dough, divide it into 8 portions, and roll each into a rope shape.
6. Form each rope into a pretzel shape.
7. Boil water with baking soda, and drop the pretzels in for 30 seconds each.
8. Place them on the baking sheet, and bake for 12-15 minutes until golden brown.

Flatbread

Ingredients:

- 2 cups (250g) all-purpose flour
- 1 tsp salt
- 1 tsp baking powder
- 1/2 cup (120ml) warm water
- 2 tbsp olive oil

Instructions:

1. In a bowl, combine flour, salt, and baking powder.
2. Add warm water and olive oil, mixing until the dough forms.
3. Knead for 5-7 minutes, then divide the dough into 6 pieces.
4. Roll each piece into a thin circle.
5. Heat a skillet over medium heat and cook each flatbread for 2-3 minutes per side, until golden.
6. Serve warm.

Pumpernickel Bread

Ingredients:

- 1 1/2 cups (190g) rye flour
- 1 1/2 cups (190g) all-purpose flour
- 1 packet (2 1/4 tsp) active dry yeast
- 1 1/4 cups (300ml) warm water
- 2 tbsp molasses
- 1 tsp salt
- 1 tbsp vegetable oil

Instructions:

1. In a bowl, combine rye flour, all-purpose flour, yeast, and salt.
2. Add warm water, molasses, and oil, mixing until the dough comes together.
3. Knead for 8-10 minutes until smooth.
4. Let rise for 1-2 hours.
5. Shape into a loaf, let rise for 30 minutes, then bake at 350°F (175°C) for 30-40 minutes.

Amish White Bread

Ingredients:

- 3 cups (375g) all-purpose flour
- 1 packet (2 1/4 tsp) active dry yeast
- 1 tbsp sugar
- 1 tsp salt
- 1 1/4 cups (300ml) warm water
- 2 tbsp vegetable oil

Instructions:

1. Combine flour, yeast, sugar, and salt in a large bowl.
2. Add warm water and oil, mixing until dough forms.
3. Knead for 8-10 minutes.
4. Let rise for 1-2 hours, shape into a loaf, and place in a greased pan.
5. Let rise again for 30-45 minutes, then bake at 375°F (190°C) for 30-35 minutes. Let cool before serving.

Artisan Bread

Ingredients:

- 3 1/2 cups (440g) all-purpose flour
- 1 1/2 tsp salt
- 1 packet (2 1/4 tsp) active dry yeast
- 1 1/2 cups (360ml) warm water
- 1 tbsp olive oil

Instructions:

1. In a large bowl, mix flour, salt, and yeast.
2. Add warm water and olive oil, stirring until a dough forms.
3. Knead the dough for 8-10 minutes until smooth.
4. Place dough in a lightly greased bowl, cover, and let rise for 1-2 hours, until doubled.
5. Preheat oven to 450°F (230°C) and place a baking stone or sheet in the oven.
6. Punch down the dough, shape it into a round loaf, and let it rest for 30 minutes.
7. Slash the top with a sharp knife.
8. Bake for 30-35 minutes until golden brown. Let cool before serving.

Herb Bread

Ingredients:

- 3 cups (375g) all-purpose flour
- 1 tsp salt
- 2 tsp dried rosemary
- 1 tsp dried thyme
- 1 packet (2 1/4 tsp) active dry yeast
- 1 cup (240ml) warm water
- 1 tbsp olive oil

Instructions:

1. In a bowl, combine flour, salt, rosemary, thyme, and yeast.
2. Add warm water and olive oil, stirring to form dough.
3. Knead for 8-10 minutes until smooth.
4. Let dough rise in a greased bowl for 1-2 hours.
5. Punch down dough, shape into a loaf, and place it on a baking sheet.
6. Let rise for 30 minutes. Preheat oven to 375°F (190°C).
7. Bake for 25-30 minutes until golden. Let cool before slicing.

Sweet Brioche Rolls

Ingredients:

- 2 cups (250g) all-purpose flour
- 1/2 cup (100g) sugar
- 1 packet (2 1/4 tsp) active dry yeast
- 1/2 tsp salt
- 1/2 cup (120ml) warm milk
- 1/2 cup (115g) butter, softened
- 2 large eggs
- 1 tsp vanilla extract

Instructions:

1. In a bowl, combine flour, sugar, yeast, and salt.
2. In another bowl, whisk together warm milk, butter, eggs, and vanilla.
3. Gradually add wet ingredients to dry ingredients and knead for 8-10 minutes.
4. Place dough in a greased bowl, cover, and let rise for 1-2 hours.
5. Punch down the dough and divide it into small rolls.
6. Place rolls in a greased pan, cover, and let rise for 30 minutes.
7. Preheat oven to 350°F (175°C) and bake for 20-25 minutes, until golden brown. Let cool before serving.

Lemon Bread

Ingredients:

- 2 cups (250g) all-purpose flour
- 1 tsp baking powder
- 1/2 tsp baking soda
- 1/2 tsp salt
- 1 cup (200g) sugar
- 1/2 cup (120ml) milk
- 2 large eggs
- 1/2 cup (115g) butter, softened
- 1 tbsp lemon zest
- 1/4 cup (60ml) fresh lemon juice

Instructions:

1. Preheat oven to 350°F (175°C) and grease a loaf pan.
2. In a bowl, whisk together flour, baking powder, baking soda, and salt.
3. In another bowl, beat sugar, milk, eggs, butter, lemon zest, and lemon juice until combined.
4. Gradually add dry ingredients to wet ingredients and mix until smooth.
5. Pour the batter into the prepared loaf pan and bake for 55-60 minutes, until a toothpick comes out clean.
6. Let cool before slicing.

Cheese Bread

Ingredients:

- 2 1/2 cups (310g) all-purpose flour
- 1 packet (2 1/4 tsp) active dry yeast
- 1 tsp salt
- 1/2 tsp garlic powder
- 1 cup (240ml) warm water
- 1 cup (120g) shredded cheddar cheese
- 1 tbsp olive oil

Instructions:

1. In a bowl, combine flour, yeast, salt, and garlic powder.
2. Add warm water and olive oil, stirring to form dough.
3. Knead for 8-10 minutes, then fold in shredded cheese.
4. Let dough rise for 1-2 hours until doubled.
5. Punch down the dough, shape it into a loaf, and place it in a greased pan.
6. Let rise for 30 minutes. Preheat oven to 375°F (190°C).
7. Bake for 25-30 minutes until golden and cheese is melted. Let cool before serving.

Olive Bread

Ingredients:

- 3 cups (375g) all-purpose flour
- 1 packet (2 1/4 tsp) active dry yeast
- 1 tsp salt
- 1 cup (240ml) warm water
- 1/2 cup (80g) pitted green or black olives, chopped
- 1 tbsp olive oil

Instructions:

1. In a bowl, combine flour, yeast, and salt.
2. Add warm water and olive oil, stirring until dough forms.
3. Knead for 8-10 minutes, then fold in chopped olives.
4. Place dough in a greased bowl, cover, and let rise for 1-2 hours.
5. Punch down the dough and shape it into a loaf.
6. Place dough on a greased baking sheet and let rise for 30 minutes.
7. Preheat oven to 375°F (190°C) and bake for 30-35 minutes until golden brown. Let cool before slicing.

Apple Cinnamon Bread

Ingredients:

- 2 cups (250g) all-purpose flour
- 1 tsp baking powder
- 1/2 tsp baking soda
- 1 tsp ground cinnamon
- 1/2 tsp salt
- 1 cup (200g) sugar
- 1/2 cup (120ml) milk
- 2 large eggs
- 1/2 cup (115g) butter, softened
- 1 cup (150g) peeled and chopped apples
- 1 tsp vanilla extract

Instructions:

1. Preheat oven to 350°F (175°C) and grease a loaf pan.
2. In a bowl, whisk together flour, baking powder, baking soda, cinnamon, and salt.
3. In another bowl, beat sugar, milk, eggs, butter, and vanilla until smooth.
4. Gradually add dry ingredients to wet ingredients, mixing until combined.
5. Gently fold in chopped apples.
6. Pour the batter into the prepared pan and bake for 50-60 minutes.
7. Let cool before slicing.

Egg Bread

Ingredients:

- 3 cups (375g) all-purpose flour
- 1 packet (2 1/4 tsp) active dry yeast
- 1 tsp salt
- 1/2 tsp sugar
- 1/2 cup (120ml) warm water
- 2 large eggs
- 1/4 cup (60g) butter, softened

Instructions:

1. In a bowl, combine flour, yeast, salt, and sugar.
2. Add warm water, eggs, and butter. Mix to form dough.
3. Knead for 8-10 minutes until smooth.
4. Let dough rise for 1-2 hours until doubled.
5. Punch down the dough, shape into a loaf, and let rise for 30 minutes.
6. Preheat oven to 350°F (175°C) and bake for 30-35 minutes, until golden. Let cool before slicing.

Anadama Bread

Ingredients:

- 2 cups (250g) cornmeal
- 2 cups (250g) all-purpose flour
- 1 packet (2 1/4 tsp) active dry yeast
- 1 tsp salt
- 1 tbsp sugar
- 1 1/2 cups (360ml) warm water
- 2 tbsp butter, softened

Instructions:

1. In a bowl, combine cornmeal, flour, yeast, salt, and sugar.
2. Add warm water and butter, mixing to form dough.
3. Knead for 8-10 minutes, then let rise for 1-2 hours.
4. Punch down the dough and shape it into a loaf.
5. Place dough in a greased loaf pan and let rise for 30 minutes.
6. Preheat oven to 375°F (190°C) and bake for 30-35 minutes. Let cool before serving.

Bialys

Ingredients:

- 2 cups (250g) all-purpose flour
- 1 packet (2 1/4 tsp) active dry yeast
- 1 tsp salt
- 1/2 cup (120ml) warm water
- 1 tbsp olive oil
- 1/2 medium onion, finely chopped
- 1/4 cup (30g) poppy seeds

Instructions:

1. In a bowl, combine flour, yeast, and salt.
2. Add warm water and olive oil, stirring to form dough.
3. Knead dough for 8-10 minutes until smooth.
4. Let dough rise for 1-2 hours until doubled in size.
5. Punch down the dough, divide into 8 portions, and form into flat rounds.
6. Preheat oven to 375°F (190°C) and place a baking sheet inside.
7. Make an indentation in the center of each round and fill with onions and poppy seeds.
8. Bake for 20-25 minutes until golden brown. Let cool before serving.

Lavash

Ingredients:

- 2 cups (250g) all-purpose flour
- 1 tsp salt
- 1/2 tsp sugar
- 1 packet (2 1/4 tsp) active dry yeast
- 1 cup (240ml) warm water
- 2 tbsp olive oil

Instructions:

1. In a bowl, combine flour, salt, sugar, and yeast.
2. Add warm water and olive oil, stirring until dough forms.
3. Knead the dough for 8-10 minutes, then let rise for 1-2 hours until doubled.
4. Punch down the dough, divide it into 4 portions, and roll each portion into a thin oval shape.
5. Preheat oven to 475°F (245°C) and bake the lavash for 5-7 minutes until golden.
6. Remove from the oven, let cool, and serve.

Empanada Dough

Ingredients:

- 2 1/2 cups (310g) all-purpose flour
- 1 tsp salt
- 1 tsp sugar
- 1/2 cup (115g) butter, cold and cubed
- 1 egg
- 1/3 cup (80ml) cold water

Instructions:

1. In a bowl, combine flour, salt, and sugar.
2. Cut in cold butter until the mixture resembles coarse crumbs.
3. Add the egg and cold water, mixing until dough forms.
4. Knead the dough for a few minutes, then wrap it in plastic wrap and refrigerate for 30 minutes.
5. Roll out the dough and cut into circles for empanadas.
6. Fill with your choice of filling, fold, and crimp edges before baking at 375°F (190°C) for 20-25 minutes until golden.

Crescent Rolls

Ingredients:

- 2 cups (250g) all-purpose flour
- 1 packet (2 1/4 tsp) active dry yeast
- 1/2 tsp salt
- 1/3 cup (80g) sugar
- 1/2 cup (120ml) warm milk
- 1/4 cup (60g) butter, softened
- 1 egg
- 1/4 cup (30g) melted butter for brushing

Instructions:

1. In a bowl, combine flour, yeast, salt, and sugar.
2. Add warm milk, butter, and egg. Mix to form a dough.
3. Knead for 8-10 minutes until smooth.
4. Let dough rise for 1-2 hours until doubled.
5. Roll out dough into a large circle and cut into wedges.
6. Roll each wedge into a crescent shape and place on a baking sheet.
7. Preheat oven to 375°F (190°C) and bake for 15-20 minutes until golden.
8. Brush with melted butter before serving.

Brioche Hamburger Buns

Ingredients:

- 2 cups (250g) all-purpose flour
- 2 tbsp sugar
- 1 packet (2 1/4 tsp) active dry yeast
- 1 tsp salt
- 1/2 cup (120ml) warm milk
- 1/4 cup (60g) butter, softened
- 2 eggs

Instructions:

1. In a bowl, combine flour, sugar, yeast, and salt.
2. Add warm milk, butter, and eggs. Mix to form dough.
3. Knead for 8-10 minutes until smooth.
4. Let dough rise for 1-2 hours.
5. Punch down dough and divide it into 8 portions. Shape into buns and place on a baking sheet.
6. Let rise for 30 minutes.
7. Preheat oven to 375°F (190°C) and bake for 15-20 minutes until golden. Let cool before serving.

Fougasse

Ingredients:

- 3 cups (375g) all-purpose flour
- 1 packet (2 1/4 tsp) active dry yeast
- 1 tsp salt
- 1 tsp sugar
- 1/4 cup (60ml) olive oil
- 1 cup (240ml) warm water
- 1 tbsp rosemary

Instructions:

1. In a bowl, combine flour, yeast, salt, and sugar.
2. Add olive oil and warm water, mixing to form dough.
3. Knead for 8-10 minutes, then let rise for 1-2 hours.
4. Punch down the dough, roll it into an oval shape, and make slashes on top.
5. Sprinkle with rosemary and let rise for 30 minutes.
6. Preheat oven to 400°F (200°C) and bake for 20-25 minutes. Let cool before serving.

Rye Rolls

Ingredients:

- 2 cups (250g) rye flour
- 2 cups (250g) all-purpose flour
- 1 packet (2 1/4 tsp) active dry yeast
- 1 tsp salt
- 1 tbsp sugar
- 1 cup (240ml) warm water
- 1 tbsp olive oil

Instructions:

1. In a bowl, combine rye flour, all-purpose flour, yeast, salt, and sugar.
2. Add warm water and olive oil, mixing to form dough.
3. Knead for 8-10 minutes, then let rise for 1-2 hours.
4. Punch down the dough, divide it into rolls, and place them on a baking sheet.
5. Let rise for 30 minutes.
6. Preheat oven to 375°F (190°C) and bake for 15-20 minutes until golden. Let cool before serving.

Chocolate Babka

Ingredients:

- 3 cups (375g) all-purpose flour
- 1 packet (2 1/4 tsp) active dry yeast
- 1/2 tsp salt
- 1/2 cup (120ml) warm milk
- 1/2 cup (115g) butter, softened
- 1/2 cup (100g) sugar
- 2 eggs
- 1 cup (150g) dark chocolate, chopped

Instructions:

1. In a bowl, combine flour, yeast, and salt.
2. Add warm milk, butter, sugar, and eggs. Mix to form dough.
3. Knead for 8-10 minutes, then let rise for 1-2 hours.
4. Punch down the dough, roll it out, and sprinkle with chopped chocolate.
5. Roll up the dough and shape into a loaf. Let rise for 30 minutes.
6. Preheat oven to 350°F (175°C) and bake for 30-35 minutes. Let cool before serving.

Apple Bread

Ingredients:

- 2 cups (250g) all-purpose flour
- 1 tsp baking powder
- 1/2 tsp baking soda
- 1 tsp cinnamon
- 1/2 tsp salt
- 1 cup (200g) sugar
- 1/2 cup (120ml) milk
- 1/4 cup (60g) butter, softened
- 2 eggs
- 1 1/2 cups (200g) peeled and chopped apples

Instructions:

1. Preheat oven to 350°F (175°C) and grease a loaf pan.
2. In a bowl, whisk together flour, baking powder, baking soda, cinnamon, and salt.
3. In another bowl, beat sugar, milk, butter, and eggs until smooth.
4. Gradually add dry ingredients to wet ingredients and mix until smooth.
5. Gently fold in chopped apples.
6. Pour the batter into the prepared pan and bake for 50-60 minutes. Let cool before slicing.

Multigrain Rolls

Ingredients:

- 1 1/2 cups (190g) whole wheat flour
- 1 cup (125g) all-purpose flour
- 1/2 cup (60g) rolled oats
- 1/4 cup (30g) sunflower seeds
- 1/4 cup (30g) flaxseeds
- 1 tbsp honey
- 1 packet (2 1/4 tsp) active dry yeast
- 1 tsp salt
- 1/2 cup (120ml) warm water
- 2 tbsp olive oil
- 1/4 cup (60ml) milk (dairy or non-dairy)

Instructions:

1. In a bowl, combine the whole wheat flour, all-purpose flour, oats, sunflower seeds, flaxseeds, and salt.
2. In a separate bowl, combine warm water, honey, and yeast. Let it sit for 5-10 minutes until foamy.
3. Add the yeast mixture and olive oil to the dry ingredients. Mix to form a dough.
4. Knead the dough for 8-10 minutes, then place it in a greased bowl, cover, and let it rise for 1-2 hours.
5. Punch down the dough, divide it into 8 portions, and shape them into rolls.
6. Place the rolls on a greased baking sheet and let them rise for 30 minutes.

7. Preheat oven to 375°F (190°C) and bake for 15-18 minutes until golden. Let cool before serving.

Gluten-Free Bread

Ingredients:

- 2 cups (240g) gluten-free all-purpose flour
- 1 packet (2 1/4 tsp) active dry yeast
- 1 tsp salt
- 1 tbsp sugar
- 1 cup (240ml) warm water
- 2 tbsp olive oil
- 1 tsp apple cider vinegar
- 2 eggs

Instructions:

1. In a bowl, combine the gluten-free flour, yeast, salt, and sugar.
2. In a separate bowl, whisk together warm water, olive oil, apple cider vinegar, and eggs.
3. Pour the wet ingredients into the dry ingredients and stir until a dough forms.
4. Let the dough rest for 5 minutes.
5. Preheat the oven to 350°F (175°C) and grease a loaf pan.
6. Transfer the dough to the loaf pan, smooth the top, and let it rise for 30 minutes.
7. Bake for 30-35 minutes, until the top is golden and a toothpick comes out clean. Let cool before slicing.

Avocado Toast Bread

Ingredients:

- 1 1/2 cups (190g) all-purpose flour
- 1 packet (2 1/4 tsp) active dry yeast
- 1 tsp salt
- 1 tbsp olive oil
- 1/4 cup (60ml) warm water
- 1 ripe avocado, mashed
- 1 tbsp lemon juice
- 1 tbsp honey

Instructions:

1. In a bowl, combine flour, yeast, and salt.
2. In a separate bowl, combine warm water, olive oil, mashed avocado, lemon juice, and honey.
3. Add the wet ingredients to the dry ingredients and mix to form dough.
4. Knead the dough for 8-10 minutes, then cover and let it rise for 1-2 hours until doubled in size.
5. Punch down the dough, shape it into a loaf, and place it in a greased loaf pan.
6. Let it rise for 30 minutes.
7. Preheat the oven to 375°F (190°C) and bake for 30-35 minutes until golden and a toothpick comes out clean. Let cool before slicing.

www.ingramcontent.com/pod-product-compliance
Lightning Source LLC
LaVergne TN
LVHW081322060526
838201LV00055B/2400